# Dressing up as a
# PIRATE

Rebekah Joy Shirley
Photography by Chris Fairclough

FRANKLIN WATTS
LONDON • SYDNEY

First published in 2011 by Franklin Watts

Copyright © 2010 Arcturus Publishing Limited

Franklin Watts
338 Euston Road
London NW1 3BH

Franklin Watts Australia
Level 17/207 Kent Street, Sydney, NSW 2000

Produced by Arcturus Publishing Limited,
26/27 Bickels Yard, 151–153 Bermondsey Street, London SE1 3HA

Series concept: Discovery Books Ltd., 2 College Street, Ludlow, Shropshire, SY8 1AN
www.discoverybooks.net
Managing Editor for Discovery Books: Laura Durman
Editor: Rebecca Hunter
Designer: Blink Media
Photography: Chris Fairclough

The author and photographer would like to acknowledge the following for their help in preparing this book:
the staff and pupils of Chad Vale Primary School, Abbie Sangha, Charlie Walker, Wasiq Ul-Islam, Amelia Adams.

A CIP catalogue record for this book is available from the British Library.

Dewey Decimal Classification Number: 646.4'78

ISBN 978 1 4451 0499 7

Printed in China

Franklin Watts is a division of Hachette Children's Books, an Hachette UK company.
www.hachette.co.uk

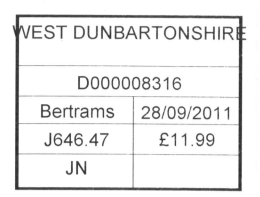

# CONTENTS

Some of the projects in this book may require the use of needles, pins and safety pins.
We would advise that young children are supervised by a responsible adult.

# TATTERED TOGS

Pirates spent most of their time at sea. Their clothes became very dirty and **tattered** because they wore them every day.

**Make your own pirate's trousers and t-shirt using:**

- A pair of old trousers
- An old t-shirt
- Coloured felt
- Fabric paints
- A marker pen
- Craft glue
- A paintbrush
- A ruler
- A pair of scissors

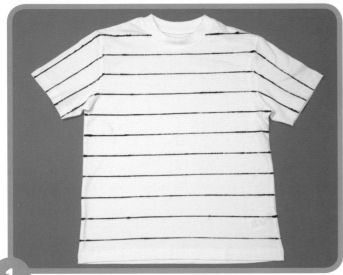

**1** Use a ruler to draw straight lines across your t-shirt.

**2** Paint every other gap with fabric paint to make the clothing stripy.

**TIP:** Put newspaper inside the t-shirt so that the paint doesn't soak through to the other side.

**3** Cut triangles along the edge of the sleeves and along the bottom of the t-shirt to make it look old and tattered.

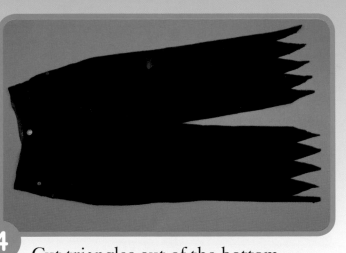

**4** Cut triangles out of the bottom of the trouser legs, too.

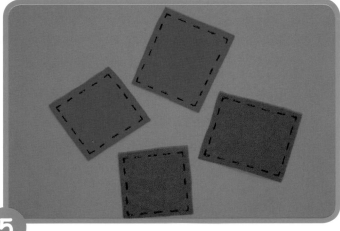

**5** Cut some 10 cm square patches out of felt. Draw stitches around the edge of the patches using fabric paint.

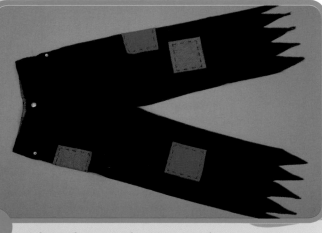

**6** Glue the patches onto the trousers using craft glue.

Now you are ready for life onboard the pirate ship. Be prepared to work hard!

# A WELL-WORN WAISTCOAT

Pirates often put on a waistcoat to look smart. Over time the waistcoat became as tatty as the pirates' other clothes.

**To make your own waistcoat you will need:**
- An old pillowcase
- A marker pen
- Fabric paint
- A paintbrush
- A pair of scissors
- A plastic bottle lid

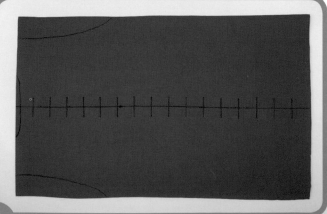

**1** Draw a straight line up the middle of the pillowcase using a marker pen. Carefully draw stitches across the line.

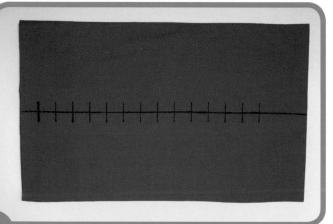

**2** Draw lines to mark the holes for your head and arms as shown in this picture.

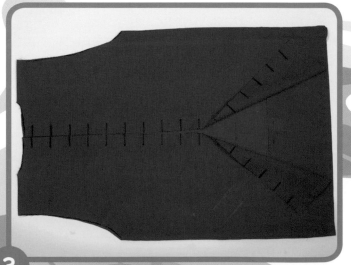

**3** Use scissors to cut along the lines to make the holes. Then cut along the middle line through the front piece of fabric only. You will then be able to open your waistcoat.

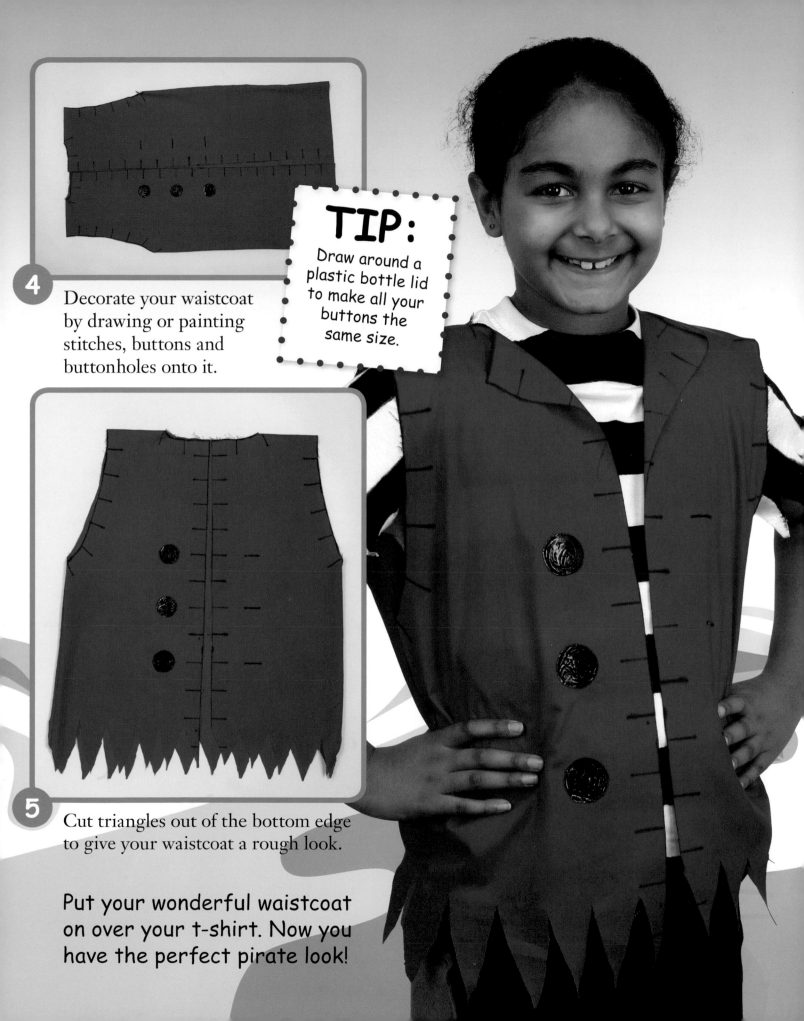

**4** Decorate your waistcoat by drawing or painting stitches, buttons and buttonholes onto it.

**TIP:** Draw around a plastic bottle lid to make all your buttons the same size.

**5** Cut triangles out of the bottom edge to give your waistcoat a rough look.

Put your wonderful waistcoat on over your t-shirt. Now you have the perfect pirate look!

# A BRILLIANT BANDANA

Pirates worked hard in the sun all day. They wore bandanas around their heads to soak up sweat.

To make a bandana you will need:
A 60 cm square piece of red fabric
A marker pen
Fabric paints
A paintbrush

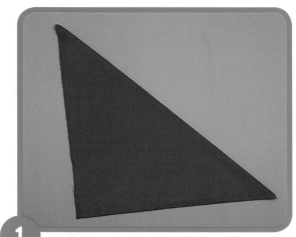

**1** Fold your red fabric in half so that it looks like a triangle.

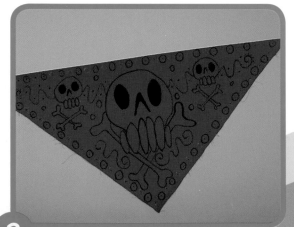

**2** Draw patterns onto the fabric using a marker pen. You could draw skulls, lines, dots or squiggles.

**3** Decorate the fabric using fabric paint.

# TIP:

## Tie your bandana like a real pirate!

Place the folded edge over your forehead. Tie the two points next to your ears together tightly at the back of your head. Tuck the third point underneath the knot.

With your bandana in place you're ready to work. But remember that pirates had lots of fun, too!

# EYE, EYE, CAPTAIN!

Pirates were a **rowdy** bunch and often had fights. If pirates **injured** an eye, they would wear an eyepatch.

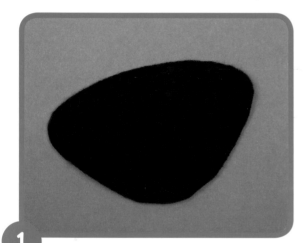

**1** Cut a rounded triangle out of felt.

**2** Fold 1 cm of the right-hand corner over. Snip a small slit in the middle of the fold.

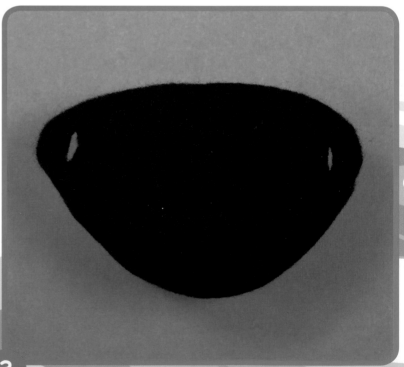

**3** Repeat step two with the left-hand corner.

**4** Wrap a piece of elastic around your head to measure the length you need. Remove the elastic from your head and cut it to length. Then thread the elastic through the slits and knot it at each end.

With your eyepatch in place, you'll look like a really tough pirate!

# HATS OFF TO PIRATES

Pirate chiefs wore hats showing the skull and crossbones to scare their enemies – and their crew!

**TIP:**
If you don't have sugar paper, you could use thin card.

**Make your own hat using:**
A2 black sugar paper
A tape measure
A pair of scissors
Sticky tape
Thin black card
A pen or pencil
A craft knife
White paint
Sponge
Gold Ribbon
Craft glue
A paintbrush

**1** Fold the sugar paper into a long strip. Measure around your head with a tape measure and cut the strip to the right length. Tape the ends together.

**2** Cut two wide, rounded triangles out of thin black card. They should be about 42 cm long.

**TIP:**
The eye sockets in the stencil must join the outer edge.

**3** Draw a skull and crossbones onto card to make a stencil. Ask an adult to help you cut it out using a craft knife.

Now that you've finished making your pirate hat, you'd better get used to bossing people around. Only the fiercest pirate chiefs can wear hats like this one.

**4** Sponge white paint through the stencil onto one of the rounded triangles.

**5** Glue gold ribbon around the edges of the triangle.

**6** Use glue or sticky tape to attach the triangles to the sugar paper ring. Glue the edges of the rounded triangles together, too.

# BY HOOK OR BY CROOK

Accidents on board ship were also **common**. If you were out at sea and lost a hand, it would be replaced with a hook.

**1** Ask an adult to cut off the top of the plastic bottle. Using glue, cover it in pieces of newspaper. Make sure you cover the sharp edge.

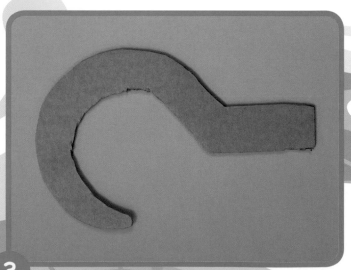

**3** Draw a hook shape on a piece of cardboard. Draw a strip underneath the hook that is 9 cm long and the same width as the bottleneck. Cut the shape out.

**2** When the glue is dry, paint the bottle black.

14

It's not easy using a hook instead of your hand. A pirate's life was hard!

**4** Paint the hook silver.

**TIP:** Make sure that the handle reaches down into the bottle top so that you can hold onto it.

**5** Push the strip into the bottleneck. Cover the join with newspaper dipped in glue. When the glue dries, paint over the join.

**6** Glue string in a zigzag at the bottom of the bottle top. Push split pins in between the string to look like gold studs.

# A PIRATE'S FEATHERED FRIEND

Life could be lonely at sea. Pirates used to keep parrots to entertain them on long **voyages**.

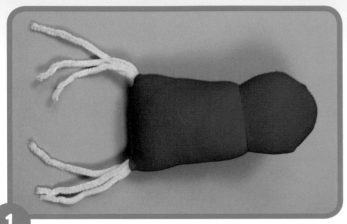

**1** Stuff the sock with tights or socks to make the parrot's body. Place three pipe cleaners at the bottom. Glue the gap to hold the pipe cleaners in place.

**TIP:**
You might need to add an extra pipe cleaner to make the ring big enough.

**3** Cut a mask shape out of a piece of felt. It should be around 10 cm wide. Cut a 10 cm **semicircle** out of yellow felt. Glue plastic eyes onto the mask. Then glue the middle of the semicircle onto the mask between the eyes.

**2** Bend the pipe cleaners around to make a ring that is big enough to fit onto your shoulder. Twist the pipe cleaners together.

**4**  Fold the semicircle and glue the sides together to make a beak. Glue the mask onto the parrot's head.

**5**  Glue colourful feathers onto the back of the parrot's body.

**6**  Cut wing shapes out of felt in different sizes and colours. Glue the shapes on top of each other.

You'll never be lonely with Polly the Parrot to keep you company. Perhaps you could teach her to say your name!

**7**  Glue the wings onto the parrot's body.

**8**  Twist two pipe cleaners around the ring. Shape them to make the parrot's feet.

# LAND AHOY!

Pirates needed to see into the distance. They used a telescope to spot faraway lands and enemy ships **approaching**.

**To make your own telescope you will need:**
- Thin black card
- A pair of scissors
- A ruler
- Gold paint
- A paintbrush
- A hole punch
- Split pins
- Craft glue

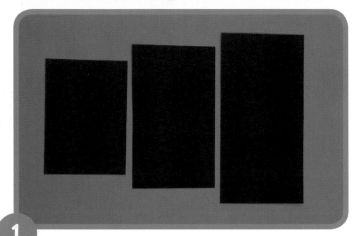

**1** Cut three rectangles out of thin black card. The first rectangle should be 14 cm x 10 cm, the second 16 cm x 10 cm and the third 18 cm x 10 cm.

**2** Paint a gold strip that is 1 cm wide along the longest edges of each rectangle.

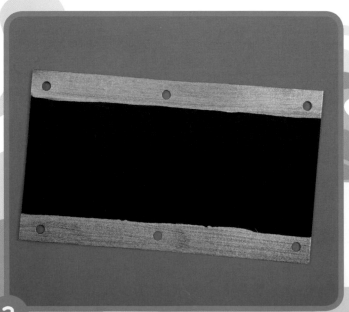

**3** Punch three holes along each long edge of the medium-sized rectangle.

Now you can see for miles and miles! When you spot land, remember to shout 'Land ahoy!'

**4** Punch three holes along one long edge of the smallest and largest rectangles.

**5** Roll each rectangle into a tube so the holes match up. Glue in place.

**TIP:** Use clothes pegs to hold the tubes in place while the glue dries.

**6** Join the three tubes together by pushing gold split pins through the holes.

# A TRUSTY CUTLASS

Pirates loved to fight! One of their favourite weapons was a curved sword called a cutlass.

**1** The cardboard tube will be your cutlass handle. Paint a 7 cm length with glue and wind string around it.

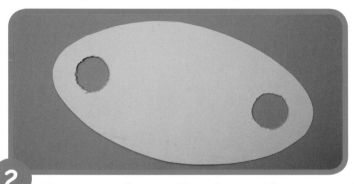

**2** Cut an **oval** out of card to make a **guard**. The oval should be around 25 cm wide. Draw around the cardboard tube and cut holes at each end of the oval.

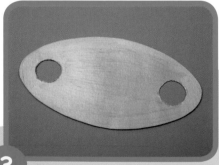

**3** Paint the guard gold.

**4** Thread the tube through the holes in the guard.

**5** Push a plastic bottle lid onto one end of the tube and glue in place.

Now that you have your cutlass, you're ready to be a fearsome pirate. Just be careful who you pick a fight with – pirates can be really mean!

**6** Draw the shape of your blade onto cardboard. The narrow end should not be wider than the cardboard tube.

**7** Cut the blade out and paint it silver.

**TIP:** Use clothes pegs to hold the blade in place while the glue dries.

**8** Cut two lines down the sides of the cardboard tube above your guard. Push your blade inside and glue in place. Cover any gaps with newspaper and glue. Paint when dry.

# X MARKS THE SPOT

Pirates buried their treasure to keep it secret from other pirates. They made maps to help them find the **booty** again when they needed it.

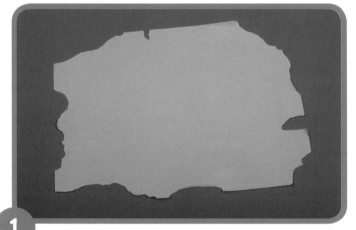

**1** Tear the edges of the paper to make it look old.

**2** Stain the paper by rubbing a cold, wet teabag over it. Let it dry.

**3** Draw a map of the island where your treasure is buried. You could draw some mountains and trees on the island, and a compass so you know which direction is north.

**4** Mark your treasure with a red X.
Draw a path to the treasure, too.

Keep your treasure
map somewhere safe,
where no other pirates
will ever find it!

# GLOSSARY

**approaching** coming towards you
**booty** a pirate word for treasure
**common** something that happens often
**guard** something that protects you
**injured** hurt or damaged
**oval** egg shaped
**semicircle** half a circle
**rowdy** noisy and rough
**tattered** torn and ragged
**voyage** a long journey at sea

# FURTHER INFORMATION

*Pirates Fun Activities* by Oscar Seaworthy (Barefoot Books, 2008)
*Pirates of the Storm* by Enid Richemont and Andy Hammond (Franklin Watts, 2010)
*Up Close: Pirates* by Paul Harrison (Franklin Watts, 2010)

http://pirateannie.fateback.com
This website is full of fun pirate activities, stories and information.
www.nationalgeographic.com/features/97/pirates/maina.html
Visit this website to go on a high seas adventure.
www.talklikeapirate.com/juniorpirates.html
This website contains lots of information about pirates, including how to talk like one!

# INDEX